HOW TO GET A I
SLEEP ALL N

By Ana Leblanc

PREFACE

How do I get my baby to sleep? This common and fre□uently asked question by new mums, comes with many others. Such as, 'Am I feeding my baby enough?', 'Why do I feel blue?', 'How am I going to get everything done today?'.

Becoming a new mum is an exciting time, it can also be somewhat challenging and difficult at times, which a lot of new mums don't anticipate.

After speaking to many a new mum over the years issues that most commonly arose where these: 'Everything was fine in the hospital, but once I got home... 'I am struggling with breast feeding', I don't have any outside support', 'I want information but I don't know where to start to look', How do I get my baby to sleep?'.

All parents would love if they could get their babies to sleep at night, instead of during the day. Although, babies sleeping schedule is all over the place by sleeping during the morning, day, afternoon, and at night, it is possible to get our little ones to go to bed at a reasonable hour. If we can get them to fall asleep at night, and wake up in the morning we could get a lot more done during the day, and a lot more sleep. It may take time, but it is possible. Find out how you can get your baby to fall asleep all night, consider all the tips hignlighted in this book and you and your child will begin to have enough sleep so both of you can become more healthier and happier.

Table of Contents

CHAPTER 1- WHY YOUR BABY IS NOT SLEEPING

Newborns are so cute, but newborn sleep can sometimes seem downright ugly! Ask any parent of a newborn, and he or she will likely tell you that long, deep, peaceful sleep is NOT on the list of things their family is enjoying.

And that's usually normal. Newborns aren't supposed to sleep 8 hours straight at night; their little bodies simply aren't designed to work that way at first. But sometimes, newborn sleeplessness can seem excessive. What do you do if your newborn seems tired, but is crying and not sleeping?

If your newborn is not sleeping, keep reading for my top tips.

Newborn Not Sleeping?

It Might Just Be Normal Newborn Sleeping Patterns.

Keep in mind that, again, newborns are supposed to wake fre□uently to feed. Indeed, your newborn's sleeping patterns are nothing like yours. It's helpful to think of newborn sleep as happening in cycles: your newborn wakes, eats, perhaps has a bit of wake time, and then goes back to sleep for anywhere from 30 minutes to 2-3 hours. This sample newborn sleep and feeding schedule (for breastfeeding babies) illustrates this cyclical sleep pattern well:

9:00 AM – Wake and Feed*

10:00 AM – Nap (30-60 minutes)

11:00 AM – Wake and Feed

12:30 PM – Nap (30-60 minutes)

1:30 PM – Wake and Feed

3:30 PM – Nap (30 – 60 minutes)

4:30 PM – Wake and Feed

6:00 PM – Nap (30 – 60 minutes)

6:30 PM – Wake and Feed

7:30 PM – Catnap (20 – 30 minutes)

8:00 PM – Wake and Feed

9:30 PM – Catnap (20 – 30 minutes)

10:00 PM – Wake and Feed

11:30 PM – Feed and Bedtime*

3:30 AM – Feed and Right back to sleep

6:30 AM – Feed and Right back to sleep

Newborn Not Sleeping? These 6 Reasons May Explain Why.

So you can expect your newborn to wake often — but if your newborn seems tired and can't fall asleep, and is instead becoming more and more upset, you no doubt want to help your newborn sleep any way you can. To do that, you'll need to pinpoint the cause of your newborn's distress and offer help as best you can.

These are, in my experience, the top 6 reasons why newborns who are tired sometimes struggle to fall asleep:

Your newborn is hungry.

This is the reason many of us jump to first when a newborn won't sleep – and it may very well be the most common cause for of a newborn not sleeping. Newborns have small tummies and therefore need to eat fre□uently; what's more, during a growth spurt, your newborn may feed what seems like every hour! So if your newborn seems distressed and won't fall asleep, try offering a feeding.

Your newborn is overtired.

If hunger is the reason many parents jump to first when their newborns won't sleep, overtiredness may be the last. But it's true; newborns can simply become too tired to fall asleep easily. The "cure" for overtiredness is simply to watch your newborn's sleep cues closely; as soon as your newborn starts showing signs of tiredness (by rubbing her eyes, yawning, looking away from your face, etc.), get her down for sleep uickly.

Your newborn is overstimulated.

A little stimulation is good for your newborn; during his wake time, it's a great idea to engage him in a story, or a few simple play activities. However, too much stimulation can stress your newborn out! Newborns don't always cope well with bright lights, loud voices, and lots of "in your face" activity. If your newborn is looking away from people and beginning to fuss, try to get your baby to a quiet area and start working towards falling asleep.

Your newborn's moro (or "startle") reflex is making it impossible to fall asleep.

You've probably observed this in your newborn before: your baby starts to fall asleep and then suddenly "startles" herself awake. Frustrating, especially if you've worked to get your baby drowsy enough to fall asleep in the first place! Fortunately, there's an age-old remedy for newborns who startle themselves awake: swaddling. If you aren't already, try swaddling your baby to help her fall asleep and stay asleep.

Your newborn is uncomfortable.

This one can be harder to pin down. If you can't seem to figure out why else your baby may be crying instead of sleeping, look to comfort. Is your newborn's diaper wet or dirty? Is your baby too warm or too cold? (In my experience, most people overdress their babies, so too warm is usually more likely.) Is your baby ill? These can all make it tough for your newborn to settle in and fall asleep.

You aren't consistent in your approach

It's easy to get off-track when you are frustrated or tired. Sometimes you might use overly-stimulating soothing techniques. Other times -- when it seems that nothing works -- you might withdraw from your baby altogether (France and Blampied 1999). It's human nature, but it's confusing for the baby, and it can make infant sleep problems worse.

To help avoid this scenario, take the time to create a single, consistent approach to your infant sleep problems. Research the science of infant sleep patterns, and decide what approach is best for you and your baby. Thinking things through ahead of time will help you stick to the plan, and may have additional psychological benefits for you. Parenting studies suggest that getting informed can boost your sense of competence and confidence, and protect you from feelings of frustration and despair (Heerman et al 2017).

Your baby's bedtime is too early -- or too late

When should babies go to bed? It can be hard to figure out. Some parents overestimate infant sleep requirements, or try to force bedtime on an infant that isn't sleepy. That's bad for a couple of reasons. In the short-term, the baby resists bedtime and everyone is unhappy. In the long-term, your child is learning to associate bedtime with the failure to fall asleep. It could be a recipe for developing bedtime resistance and insomnia (LeBourgeois et al 2013).

Other parents might be fooled by babies that seem active and energetic. If they won't settle down, isn't that proof that they don't need to sleep yet? Possibly, but they could also be hyper-reactive -- strung out or "overtired." Their stress response systems may be stuck on "high," overriding the physiological responses that would ordinarily allow them to become drowsy.

If overtiredness is the problem, pick an earlier bedtime, and help your baby wind down by introducing some soothing, low-key bedtime rituals.

Your newborn needs YOU!

It's true, parents – sometimes, your newborn simply needs to be held and cuddled by you! Just as your newborn nourishment, warmth, shelter, and sleep, he needs YOU! If your newborn is not sleeping and seems very upset, try cuddling your newborn skin-to-skin against your chest; you'll be amazed at how □uickly and effectively this can calm your newborn.

5 Wrong Beliefs About Babies and Sleep

New parents often have a hard time putting their little bundles of joy to sleep. As parents, it is their responsibility to care for their little ones. Because of this, they will do everything possible to find ways to effectively put their little angels to sleep. Of course, it will surely help if you have the ideal mattresses for them like the Sealy Baby Ultra Rest mattress, Sealy Perfect Rest crib mattress, etc. However, putting little tots to sleep isn't that simple.

In order to send the tots off to dreamland, parents go online to read up on tips and they also ask their friends and family members for help. Unfortunately, this leads to many of them believing several misconceptions. Believing in false information will not help their case. Here are five of the many wrong beliefs about infants and sleep:

Wrong Belief #1: A ⬜uiet environment will make the baby sleep.

Many parents believe that a ⬜uiet environment is a good guarantee that their babies will fall asleep. Unfortunately, this is a myth born on the personal preference of parents. In reality, some babies will feel disconcerted about the ⬜uiet and that the baby will definitely wake up. A ⬜uiet environment is not a guarantee that a baby will fall asleep.

Wrong Belief #2: Babies will continue to sleep through the night and wake up when morning comes especially if you tire them out during the day.

Another misconception given by the fact that parents think that their infants sleep just like they do is the one where they actually think that once they're tucked in bed, they will sleep until morning comes. If they believe this, then they are just setting themselves up for disappointment. Young ones will wake up whenever they want to. This includes even during the wee hours of the morning.

Wrong Belief #3: Never wake a sleeping tot.

Parents believe that waking a sleeping infant is not a good idea. This is not the right thought because in all actuality, they will just get back to sleep if they are still sleepy.

Wrong Belief #4: Feeding solid food will make them sleep longer.

Solid food only helps sleep if the person is a grown adult. Solid food will not help infants sleep longer. Parents who believe this are just wasting time. This will expain in details in subsequent chapters.

Wrong Belief # 5: Making a baby cry until he or she is tired will make him or her go to sleep.

If parents do this, they are just hurting their kids. This is because making him or her cry it out to sleep just wears the baby's vocal chords. Parents should pacify their children when they cry.

The only thing that parents should have in mind is that babies will sleep whenever they feel like. This is why they should adjust to their baby's sleeping patterns and not the other way around. Of course, because tots need a lot of sleep, it's recommended to make sure they get a comfy bed. That's the reason why choosing the right crib mattresses matters.

CHAPTER 2- UNDERSTANDING BABY SLEEPING PATTERN

Getting used to having a newborn baby can be difficult for parents. The most problematic adjustment for most parents can be getting accustomed to baby sleep patterns. It's no secret that a new parent can expect many sleepless nights, so understanding what type of sleep their baby will be getting might help parents to realize what these first few months will be like.

A newborn baby, for the most part, does little more than sleep and feed. This keeps mother busy with breast-feeding and diaper changes around the clock. Baby sleep patterns for the first 3 weeks should be a total of 16-20 hours of sleep every day. Since they will only sleep for about 2 hours at a time, this means parents will only be able to take short naps for the first three weeks, or will need to sleep in shifts. At 3 weeks, baby will begin sleeping 16 to 18 hours per day, perhaps sleeping for longer periods. At 6 weeks, the baby will sleep even less, around 15 to 16 hours a day total. This means parents could expect to sleep a little more at this age.

The age of four months means baby will be sleeping 9 to 12 hours at night plus 2 naps during the day. Parents will rejoice as baby sleep patterns finally allow them to have a full night's sleep. Over the next few months, baby will continue to have more stable sleep patterns and give parents a much-needed break from interrupted sleep. These baby sleep patterns are necessary for baby to get the food and comfort she needs to develop normally. Making sure to understand what to expect at different stages can help prepare the new parents for the sleep they will be able to get as baby grows.

Baby sleeping pattern during their 3-6 months old varies from one to another. Although, babies at the age of 3-6 months are able to sleep longer at night, this doesn't mean you should suddenly apply a rigid sleep program on your baby at 3-4 months old.

In fact, your baby may already have developed their own sleeping patterns. Some may just sleep 6 hours during the night and have about 3-5 hours nap in the afternoon, some may sleep 12 hours straight with some short naps during the day, and with breastfed babies, some may have regular sleep and wake time to get fed more. This may not sound so much relieving if you're hoping for sudden eight or nine hours of sleep for yourself. But it's an important milestone for you as well as your baby, and by 6 months or before, your baby will be likely to be ready for night long sleep.

Many parents might ask, what would be the normal sleeping for my baby (between 3-6 months old)? The answer is there is no "normal" sleeping pattern in your 3-6 month old baby. If you are happy with your baby's sleep pattern, there is no need to change it. There are many ways to be 'normal'. But if you'd like to develop longer sleeping and keep more regular hours on your baby, now might be a good time to try some type of sleep training. Always remember that every baby is uni☐ue one another in developmental schedule. See how your child reacts to the sleep training, and if he doesn't seem ready, slow down and try again in a few weeks.

It sure takes time, but by 3-6 months most babies will "understand" that nighttime is for sleeping and are able to sleep for 6-12 hour stretches.

This must be great news to parents who are usually very exhausted by this stage and looking for a break!

You can shift Your Baby Sleep Patterns and Get More Rest Yourself

Many parents of newborns have trouble getting enough sleep. However, there are things you can do to adjust baby sleep patterns, so that you can get more rest. You can emphasize the idea that daytime is for activities, while nighttime is for sleeping. You can also watch out for early warning signs which show that your baby is already weary.

The Hard Part About Baby Sleep Patterns

Having a newborn in the house is cause for a lot of joy, as well as a lot of fatigue. The joy comes into play because the family welcomes a new member into the fold. The fatigue is there because the little one is completely dependent on you, as parents. You have to see to the baby's needs. These includes feeding, burping, bathing, cleaning, diaper changing and so much more. It's a hectic and almost frantic time, and one of the first casualties of varying baby sleep patterns is your own ability to get a good night's rest.

Early Baby Sleep Patterns

However, this is not something that you have to take lying down. It is possible to understand the sleeping patterns of your little one and adjust them to be more in line with adult sleeping patterns. What has been found out is that babies end up sleeping for a very large fraction of the day. In fact, they're generally asleep for two-thirds of the day.

The problem though is that they only usually stay asleep for short periods of time. Unlike adults who can remain asleep for eight straight hours or longer, babies will tend to remain asleep for only up to four hours at a time. This means that there is a fundamental incompatibility between the sleeping patterns of newborns and adults, which results in babies waking up their parents repeatedly.

How to Shift Baby Sleeping Patterns

There are things that parents can do so that, over time, the little one will tend to sleep during the evening and stay awake during the day. One way to do this is by emphasizing to your baby the fact that daytime is for staying active, while nighttime is for sleeping. To do this, you can make sure that the interior of the house is getting sufficient natural light during the day, and is on the darker side at night. You can also more actively play with your baby during the day, while being more laid back and relaxed at night.

Another thing you can do is observe your baby carefully throughout the day and night, watching for early warning signs which show that he or she is already weary. The goal is to make sure that when your baby is already tired, you are able to let your little one nap. What you want to avoid is continuing to stimulate or actively play with your baby, when he or she is already tired. This is one of those things which tends to mess with your little one's sleeping patterns.

How Long Should My Baby Sleep For?

New born babies will usually sleep 16 to 17 hours a day. Usually, a baby will not sleep all the way through a night until they reach the age of 3 months. There are a couple of reasons why this is the case. The first is that they have small stomachs, so they become hungry a lot quicker, particularly if they are breastfed. It is easier for them to digest breast milk than to digest formula, so they will have to eat more often, particularly at the start of their lives.

They also sleep in shorter cycles and dream in shorter cycles than adults do. Most of the time, new born babies sleep an average of 8 hours a day and 8 hours a night. They won't sleep 8 hours straight, though. When you first bring them home, they will sleep in very short cycles.

Until your baby reaches 2 years old, he or she will sleep 13 to 14 hours, but they will sleep less during the day as they get older. When your baby reaches the age of 2, he should be able to sleep all through the night and take a nap for 2 hours in the day. Keep in mind that baby sleep patterns are different for each baby, so yours might need to take two naps or one long nap. When they reach this age, try to get them to take their naps early because if they take a nap too late, they might not want to fall asleep at night.

When your baby starts to sleep all the way through the night, you might be frustrated when they start waking up again in the middle of the night. Most of the time, this occurs when they are about 6 months old and means that they are experiencing a normal development called separation anxiety.

Of course, the above figures are just a guide. Don't be concerned if this pattern does not seem to fit your newborn. Sleep needs vary a lot between individual babies and it is not beneficial to compare your newborn's sleep patterns with others.

CHAPTER 3- WHEN SHOULD I PUT MY BABY TO BED?

In the first few weeks of your baby's life, having any sort of bedtime routine is pretty much impossible. Her body clock is yet to kick in, and many babies are virtually nocturnal.

When will you ever get to eat a meal with your husband again, let alone a hot one, you may ask. Will you ever be able to put your feet up and watch EastEnders all the way through?

The answer is yes!

Babies love routine – it's just a □uestion of knowing when and how to get into a bedtime one that can be tricky.

Read on for a helping hand ...

When should I start a bedtime routine

After what can be an unpredictable and relentless first few weeks with your baby, you may start to notice some patterns forming.

Of course, every baby is different (otherwise this parenting lark would be a whole lot easier!) but generally speaking you'll notice this around the three-month mark.

It may become easier to predict when your baby is likely to sleep, and finally, there are fewer evenings where you're pacing the floor in a vain attempt to send her off to the land of nod.

At this point, introducing a bedtime routine can help make sure your baby gets the sleep he needs, and give you a bit of a break too.

Why start a bedtime routine?

It may seem hard to believe if you're struggling with broken nights and are so tired you could sleep on a washing line, but by the age of two, your child will have spent half her life asleep. And there are good reasons why she needs so much shut-eye.

Sleep is essential for your baby's growth and development. It helps her nervous system develop, and means that she spends more of her waking hours in a state of alertness, where she's calm, interacting and learning all the time.

When naps and night-time sleep are unpredictable, it can make it harder for your baby to fall asleep or stay asleep. This can lead to her becoming overtired and stressed.

It's when they're asleep that babies produce the growth hormones that are so important for their normal development.

Sleep helps to boost their immune system, too.

A simple bedtime routine is often the key to helping your baby to sleep well.

Following the same steps each time, you put him to bed can help to regulate her body clock, with the difference between light and dark helping to establish a regular sleep-wake schedule.

Implementing a regular bedtime might feel like a real milestone – and that's because it is, so yay for you! Even if you were a fly-by-the-seat-of-your-pants kinda gal pre-baby, most of us appreciate a little bit of time in the day that's just for us, even if we're just sorting the washing or unloading the dishwasher: at least we can finish the job unhindered!

When routines aren't right

Of course, if you don't want to be bound by the rigidity of a routine, or think enforcing it is going to make you stressed, don't feel under pressure to start one.

You might decide you'd rather keep your baby up later so your partner can spend some time with him after work. Or maybe you co-sleep and don't fancy having to go to bed with your baby at 7.30pm.

As long as you and your baby are both getting enough sleep to function, go with what suits you and your family best.

What your bedtime routine involves is entirely up to you, but the aim is to help your baby gradually wind down so that by the time you switch the lights out, he's ready to sleep. It might include:

A baby massage

A bath

Changing her into a sleepsuit or pajamas

Brushing her teeth

Dimming the lights in the nursery

Giving her a final feed

Reading a bedtime story

Singing a lullaby or putting on her musical mobile

Putting her into bed, making sure you're following safe sleep guidance like laying her on his back, with her feet at the foot of the cot if you use blankets

Saying goodnight using a set phrase, such as, 'night night, sleep tight'

The idea is that if you repeat the same steps night after night, your baby will begin to recognize that it's time to sleep.

Bring on the peaceful evenings ...

Top tips for a bedtime routine that works

Turn off the TV: the Bedtime Hour might be intended to help children unwind before bed, but it can overstimulate some, and lead to a meltdown when you try to turn it off. TV interferes with the production of melatonin the sleep hormone too, making it harder to get to sleep.

Keep distractions to a minimum. By all means put your children in the bath together, but then get older siblings to do something else ⬜uietly while you settle your baby.

Make a clear difference between day and night. During the day, keep the curtains open and don't worry about tiptoeing around the house at naptime. In the evening, shut the curtains, dim the lights and keep the volume down. This will regulate your baby's body clock and help her learn that night-time is sleep time.

Be flexible. If your baby has a late nap, she might not be tired by his usual bedtime. If she got up super-early, you may need to move her bedtime forward a bit.

Aim to put your baby to bed sleepy, but not actually asleep. If she gets used to falling asleep in your arms or during a feed, she'll need you to do the same every time she wakes (and believe me, rocking a 25lb toddler to sleep is very different from rocking a newborn!).

How NOT To Put Your Baby To Sleep

Feeding Baby Until They Fall Asleep - Many, many parents make the mistake of continually feeding their baby either by breastfeeding or bottle feeding until their baby falls asleep. Some parents believe that feeding their baby lots of food before they go to sleep will help them sleep better and longer. In fact, using the method to put your baby to sleep is very unhealthy. One of the reasons it is unhealthy is that it begins a bad routine for your child, having them expect a full belly when going to sleep. Another negative of this method is that it makes your baby feel like it has to be sucking on something when it falls asleep. Last but not least, putting your child to sleep this way can also cause them to have an upset stomach and will likely result in your child sleeping in a soiled or waking in the night because of it.

Letting Baby Sleep Where They May - The title of this bullet may seem confusing to some. Let me explain. Many parents will let them baby stay up until they just pass out and never build a routine around bed time. This of course is a bad idea and not a healthy way to put your baby to sleep either. Routines are essential in a baby's growth and development. They crave routine and you should take advantage of this craving. Having a bedtime routine should include a task you do every night before bedtime. This task may be giving baby a bath using lavender scented baby shampoo, singing, reading, massaging, etc. If you make it a habit of doing a specific task with your baby each night he/she will begin to associate it with bed time. Having a routine will also help your baby settle down into their own crib, allowing baby to sleep without crying and fussing.

A Little Bit Of Cough Syrup Does The Trick - I know it sounds absurd to you, but this is much more common than you may think. Generally, when someone uses cough syrup it's not the parent. Often it is a nanny, babysitter or even a relative. They do this so the baby will go to sleep and not bother the caregiver. The parents will come home, ask about the baby and often the response is, "He/She is such a good kid. He/She has been catching up on his/her sleep." Of course this not a healthy way to put your baby to sleep, but the sad fact is some people use this horrid and disgusting techni☐ue.

When Should You Move Your Child From a Crib to a Bed?

There are no hard and fast rules on when exactly you should move your child from the crib to a bed although most make the transition between the ages of 18 to 36 months. Different children react to this transition differently with some freely giving up their crib while others stubbornly refusing to move no matter what you do.

Crib Tent

Parents too have differing views on this issue. Some feels an early transition is good as it fosters confidence and independence. On the other hand, others do not like to rush and prefer to make the transition at the last possible moment when they feel that their child is truly ready for the move. To keep their child safe in the crib, they resort to a crib tent. Although some experts deem crib tents to be hazardous as it can be difficult to get your child out in case of an emergency, it is one way of preventing your toddler from climbing out of the crib.

General Rule

Because transition to a bed may cause some toddlers to feel distraught and may result in bedtime battles, some parents tend to delay the move. However, the general rule is you should move your toddler to a bed when he or she has reached around three feet in height or shows signs of climbing out of the crib. The other good gauge is you should move your toddler when the side rails come up to less than 75% of your child's height when he or she is standing in the crib.

One other □uestion you should ask yourself is whether your child is potty-trained and maybe better off sleeping on a bed to enable him or her to get up and use the toilet as and when necessary.

Readiness

The other view is you should assess your child's readiness first before deciding when to move him or her from the crib to a bed. Therefore, you do not need to rush out and buy a toddler bed the moment your child shows signs of climbing out of the crib. This is because being able to climb out of the crib does not mean he or she is ready for a bed. Not all toddlers can sleep soundly throughout the night on their own and it may be equally dangerous to have your child roaming the house in the middle of the night when you are fast asleep.

Bear in mind that your toddler can easily get on and off a toddler bed once you make him or her move out of the crib. You would have to assess the risk of keeping your toddler in a crib as well as shifting him to a bed and put in place safety measures to guard against injury. The above are just some of the factors you should consider when confronted with the issue of transition.

Free Up The Crib

One other common reason parents move their child to a bed is because they need to free up the crib for the new baby. However, to force your child out of the crib to accommodate a new baby will only cause resentment in the process. If you really need to get your toddler out of the crib for the new baby, try to do so weeks before your baby is due. This way, your toddler is less likely to feel that he or she has to give up the crib for the new baby. Otherwise, you may be better off getting another crib, especially if you know your toddler just isn't ready for a bed.

While there is no necessity to rush your child to a bed, there is also little reason to delay the transition when the need arises. A way to help your toddler along with the move is to ease him or her into the idea before it becomes absolutely necessary to make the transition for obvious safety reasons. By doing so, your child would be less likely to reject the new bed as the move does not seem sudden and forced.

CHAPTER 4-HOW DO I GET MY BABY TO SLEEP ALL NIGHT

Having a new baby is exciting, but it can also be overwhelming and leave new parents sleep deprived. Some babies sleep through the night right away and others don't get to that point until they are a year old or more. This is a very long time for parents to go without a good night of sleep. There are some things you can do to get your baby to sleep through the night.

Most infants are able to sleep for six hours or more at night by the time they are six months old as their nervous system matures. It is important to keep your baby on a regular schedule as much as possible. This includes a bedtime ritual. Give your baby a bath, read a story, cuddle, and put them to bed. Your child will get used to this bedtime ritual. While it is common to rock a baby to sleep, it is important that you lay your child down for bedtime while they are still awake. This allows them to associate the night time routine with falling asleep.

Most babies can sleep through the night if they are comfortable. Make sure your baby is getting enough to eat. If your baby is waking up at night to eat, give him or her a feeding of cereal, pudding, or other filling food item that is appropriate for their age. This will help them stay full to sleep for a long stretch of time at night. To keep your baby comfortable through the night without a diaper change, use thick absorbent diapers for bed time. Make sure you put on baby power to prevent a rash or skin irritation from occurring.

If your baby does wake up at night to be changed or fed, do so very ⬜uietly and calmly. Keep the lighting very dim. If your child becomes stimulated then they will likely want to stay awake. Once you have fed and changed your baby, place them back into their crib so that they can easily fall back to sleep.

For babies who like to sleep too much during the day and then stay up at night, you will need to work to help them get on schedule. Keep them awake more during the day by finding stimulating activities. Cut nap time back by 10 to 15 minutes throughout the day to help them sleep better at night. Don't let your baby nap late in the afternoon or early evening. This process is going to take a couple of days, and your baby may be cranky during the process, but once it is done you will all be sleeping better.

What Every Mother Should Know About Getting A Baby to Sleep Through the Night

Your child's health is likely to be a high priority and you already know that kids get very cranky and difficult if they don't get enough sleep! As a rough guide a three month old infant needs around fifteen hours of sleep whereas a two year old need twelve to thirteen hours a day, including naps.

But if you're worried about your baby not sleeping, this is going to become an ever increasing issue between you and your baby. You will discover that getting baby to sleep through the night is a challenging task to accomplish.

If you are a new mom or dad and are losing sleep about this subject, there are some areas you should explore. The first thing is to let your child know that bedtime is special. Bedtime is the best time to show your child he is loved but at the same time structure and firmness must be maintained.

How to get baby to sleep through the night also depends on you and your approach. Spend some quality time with your baby at bedtime. It's up to you, as a parent, to set an example for your children when they aren't co-operating. So even if your little one is fussing during bedtime keep firm and organized. Establish a familiar bedtime routine that your child will come to expect. This bedtime routine means playtime is finished and it's time for sleep and nothing else. Don't break this rule even if your child puts on a temper tantrum.

Getting baby to sleep through the night is do-able so long as you stick to a regular routine. This includes the same waking, meal, nap and play times. This type of structure will help your child to feel secure and comfortable and make it easier for him to go to sleep. It's a fact of life that toddlers, as well as infants need to know what to expect.

And although you may be tempted, don't cram your baby's bed full of toys. What happens when you create the sleep space with toys is that it becomes a play area and not a sanctuary for rest and slumber. A bed full of toys will distract your baby and keep him awake. To help allay separation issues one or two transitional things such as a favorite book, blanket or stuffed animal is not so distracting.

But if all else fails and you still cannot get your child to sleep, a natural aid can be of great assistance in how to get baby to sleep through the night. There are homeopathic and herbal remedies that help soothe your child so they can get that much needed sleep, not to mention some peace yourself. The first vital step is to ensure that the product is safe and non-addictive. Chamomilla will help to cause drowsiness in babies and young children and is completely safe.

Getting baby to sleep through the night with the help from a natural substance is pretty straightforward. Some of them come in sprinkles that you can simply put on your child's tongue, and dissolve in seconds. Such herbs also make good remedies for treating digestive upsets, colic, and teething.

Easy Secrets To Help Your Baby Sleep All Night!

Check to see if your baby is hungry

First of all you should check to see if your baby is hungry. To do this with young babies simply place you finger under their chin and if it tries to suck or move toward it then it means that your baby is hungry.

Walk with your baby

Walk with your baby or sit in a rocking chair. The continuous movement will soothe your baby. However, be sure to place your baby's head close to your chest so that it can hear your heartbeat.

Burping while feeding

Try burping your baby more frequently during feeding.

Know that a colic attack is coming and be prepared for it

When dealing with a colicky baby it is best to plan ahead. For example, if your baby usually has colic attacks in the afternoon/evening then you should do most of your household chores in the morning. Make sure that if your baby has been awake for most of the morning that he/she gets a nap in the afternoon and you take one with them. A nap can actually reduce the fre□uency of the colic attacks and how long they last.

Play music

Play music like classical or slow music as some babies respond better to sound and will find it soothing.

Stop the Crying as soon as possible

Using a pacifier may help stop your baby crying however if this does not work a small bottle of sugar water helps calm and relax the baby.

Stopping your baby's crying spells as □uickly and calmly as possible can significantly shorten the episodes of colic.

Massage

Place your baby across your lap while he/she lies on his/her belly and rub his/her back. This will help get rid of air in your baby's stomach and prevent gas.

Neck nestling - Dad's are fantastic at this!

This is when the baby snuggles his/her head into the space that is located between the jaw and chest of the parent. Your jawbone drapes gently over the baby's head and your voice box presses against its' head. Small babies hear not only with their ears but also the vibrations that go through their skull. If you sing something monotonous like a lullaby it will help your baby to drift off to sleep. This technique works best with dad's because they have a lower pitch and higher vibration from their voice.

A special favourite - especially good for dad's as well!

This is a good techni□ue for dad's to do. What you have to do is drape your bare skinned but diapered baby over your bare chest. Make sure that your baby's ear is over your heartbeat. The rhythm of your heart combined with the rhythm of your chest moving as you are breathing and a bit of rhythmic patting on your baby's back will usually soothe both of you.

Use motion

Some babies prefer to be still when calmed down whereas, others like the use of motion to be soothed. Motion swings set at approximately 60 beats per minute is an excellent device to be used for those types of babies. The constant motion is great for relaxing the baby. However, you should bear in mind that for some babies this may not work as the swing only provides a back and forth motion.

A vibrating bouncer is another excellent tool to use to calm down your colicky baby. The vibration and rhythmic sound coming from this device will soothe your baby.

Caring for a colicky baby can be extremely stressful and frustrating at times but, remember it's not your fault. Also, bear in mind that you need to take care of yourself as well. You can't be very soothing to your baby if you are all tense and stressed. You need to try to relax and remember that your baby will outgrow this phase. In addition, keep in mind that if you need to take a break from your baby's crying then do so, there is nothing wrong with that. Family and relatives are often understanding and happy to take care of your baby when you need some time out for yourself, even if your baby is crying. If there is no one around it's OK to put your baby in the crib, let him/her cry and take a break before trying to make another attempt.

Do not fear or worry too much if your child has colic as your baby will outgrow it. However, do consult your doctor if your baby screams constantly or if your baby's colic attacks are accompanied with excessive vomiting, diarrhea and constipation. These symptoms may indicate a more serious problem.

CHAPTER 5- HOW TO CURE SLEEPING PROBLEMS IN BABIES

If your baby is not sleeping well, this could be due to several reasons. Some of the reasons we hear most about are colic or abdominal discomfort, food intolerance, teething, urinary tract infection or even separation anxiety. Apart from these reasons, external factors such as lack of a suitable baby bed or uncomfortable pyjamas could also keep your baby awake at night. Try to find out the reason your baby isn't sleeping well before seeking out some baby sleep help.

Many babies have problems sleeping, so you're not alone. Most of these problems will simply go away on their own as your baby gets older. Most children will outgrow these problems as they grow and mature. However, at times, sleeping problems could become chronic and could develop into more serious sleeping disorders. If your child's sleeping problems persist, ask for some baby sleep help from your doctor or pediatrician.

The first thing to do is to make sure your baby is comfortable. Arrange your baby's bed properly, make sure the room temperature is not too hot or too cold, and establish a good sleeping routine. These are really simple things, but they will go a long way in helping baby sleep peacefully. But the most important thing you should do as far as your baby's sleeping problems are concerned is choosing the right medication.

Natural remedies are the best when it comes to treating sleeping problems in babies. Babies, needless to say, are gentle and tender.

Chemical medications, though effective, could cause a lot of side effects. Most importantly, chemical medications for sleeping disorders are usually addictive. In fact, it is very risky to give these medications to your child. So, if you are looking for some good baby sleep help, go for homeopathic medications which are both powerful and safe.

There are a number of advantages of choosing homeopathic sleep medications over chemical ones. Natural remedies are very safe. There are little to no chances of side effects at all. They are ☐uite safe to use on a regular basis. They do not act as a sedative. They relax your baby's body, induce drowsiness and promote a healthy sleeping pattern.

Some of the herbal extracts present in homeopathic medications are capable of treating problems like digestive upsets, colic, irritability, and anxiety in small children. They also have a tran☐uilizing effect and help your baby sleep well.

Baby sleeping disorder

It is natural for infant's to not sleep regularly for the first few months after they arrive home. They have all new surroundings to become familiar with and must be fed and changed often. Mothers who have just brought a new baby home are all too familiar with them frequently waking at night and sleeping in short spurts. Even though this is common, infants like everyone else can have sleep disorders.

When should a parent be concerned about their child's inability to sleep? This can be hard to determine because every child is different and adjusts at different rates. On average, a new baby needs to sleep around sixteen hours a day and this gradually decreases as they get older. How many times they wake to be fed and changed also becomes less. Infant sleep disorders can be hard to detect by both parents and doctors because many of the symptoms they experience normal for infants.

Night terrors are a parasomnia that some infants can experience. A night terror will happen approximately ninety minutes after they have fallen asleep. These occurrences are much different than a regular nightmare. Children will wake from a nightmare and be able to give some details of the dream. Terrors happen when the child is in a semi-conscious state and the fear is displayed by screaming, groaning, and kicking. When they awake, they are confused and do not remember what happened or why they were scared. Most children experiencing night terrors are hard to console and it may take thirty minutes or more to get them calmed back down.

Apnea is a more serious sleep disorder that occurs in infants. This condition causes the child to snore and breathe through their mouth. The mouth breathing occurs due to normal breathing stopping. The baby will wake crying and irritable. When the condition is more severe, an infant can stop breathing. Any symptoms that could link to this type of conditions should be brought to the attention of the pediatrician. They may recommend the child being evaluated by a sleep clinic for proper treatment.

Sudden Infant Death Syndrome or SIDS is more than just a sleep problem and is a major focus of health professionals. An infant with this condition actually stops breathing while they are asleep. They do not begin breathing again on their own and need help. The cause of this condition is still unknown but some doctors believe environmental factors can make it more possible for an infant to develop SIDS. They recommend that devices are used to ensure the baby sleeps on their back and that no items are left in the crib that could cause complications.

Other issues such as bed wetting can be apparent in children of various ages. As a parent, you should become familiar with these types of infant sleep disorders and be aware of the symptoms to look for. This will help you detect any sleep problems early on so you can seek medical help. You pediatrician should be able to go over any symptoms you are seeing and determine the best way to treat the sleep issues your baby is experiencing.

It is not surprising that infants can have sleep problems. Their sleep patterns are naturally irregular and they wake frequently due to hunger and other needs. Some behaviors are very normal, but others are reason for concern and can be signs of more serious problem. Sleep disorders that occur in infants include night terrors, apnea, SIDS, and bed wetting. Being able to detect these conditions is very important and can improve your child's sleep and ability to perform daily activities.

Colic and the 5 S's

Colic, the most common disruption to babies sleep which commonly occurs during the first few months of life but usually disappears at about 4 to 5 months although it can go on for up to 12 months. Colic is where a baby cries or screams and maybe writhes for long periods of time for no apparent reason. These sessions more often occur in early evening or during and after feeding.

It is becoming widely believed after many theories in the past that colic is the baby overreacting to normal sensations taking place within the digestive processes. Just as the baby over reacts to external stimuli, such as the mother's face suddenly appearing or a sudden sound, he is overreacting to the normal reflexes that tell his body to begin emptying the stomach to make room for more food. It takes him 3 or 4 months to learn to ignore these sensations.

The change of environment One theory for a colicky or fussy baby is that the normal term for pregnancy is actually shorter than ideal and is only the length it is because of the continuing increase in the size of the brain and therefore the head. A pregnancy any longer would be dangerous for both the mother and baby. The baby is therefore "evolutionary premature" and is thrust into the relatively silent world with the sudden loss of all the hypnotic sounds, the swishing and swushing of the blood pumping through the mother's body, the comforting stroking against the uterine walls, the jiggling movements and constant warmth.

The 5 S's

There is the best evidence yet that soothing measures, which may be a harp back to the lost environment of the mother's womb, can dramatically calm the baby during fits of crying and screaming preparing him to settle for sleep. The following 5 S's is the core of the theory and work, done by Dr. Harvey Karp a Californian pediatrician. These practices have worked in studies with a 98 percent success rate when done correctly.

Swaddling - using bulky blankets loosely around head and body taking care not to overheat the baby and making sure he can flex his hips

Side or Stomach position - hold the baby on his side or stomach - when sleepy can then be laid on his back

Shushing sound - making this sound quite loudly or use recorded sound

Swinging motion - with a small jiggling movement whilst supporting the head

Sucking - using breast, clean finger or pacifier

When the key elements, swaddle, swing and shush are used correctly and in combination, they can □uickly reduce crying and promote sleep.

Milk allergy

The process above is the first steps to overcome any sleeping problems with babies but if there is still some serious screaming it's just possible that there could be a problem with food allergies, either cows milk allergy or a reaction to a property in the mother's milk. The doctor will suggest a change to the mother's diet if the baby is being breastfed or a change to a hypoallergenic formula to work out what the allergy is. If the crying is because of an allergy to cow's milk, benefits should be seen between 2 and 7 days.

Good habits

Once able to manage the sleep pattern of the baby it's important to maintain a fixed and consistent waking and bed time schedule. Being persistent with this regime is necessary in order for the baby to develop the correct sleeping habits. Having said that it's also important to put the baby down when he or she is sleepy and not when asleep. This will encourage him to learn to go to sleep keeping him in good stead as he develops.

Co-sleeping

Having the baby sleeping in bed with one or more parents hasn't been shown conclusively to be good or bad long-term, although there is some evidence to show that infants who develop sleep disorders later in life did experience co-sleeping in infancy. It must not be forgotten the importance for the mother to get as good an uninterrupted sleep as possible.

It's normal for there to be sleeping problems with babies and considering the incredible change that has recently occurred in their short lives it's no wonder as they adjust to the new sensations and learn the ways of this new world away from the hypnotic rhythms, the warmth, and safety of the mother's womb.

Is Sudden Infant Death Syndrome (SIDS) A Sleep Disorder?

SIDS is defined as "a sudden and unexpected death of an infant or young child, in which a thorough postmortem examination, and examination of the death scene, fails to demonstrate an ade□uate cause for death." It is the single most fre□uent cause of infant death, accounting for about 150 deaths a year in Canada roughly 1 in 2000 live births and 3000 deaths a year in the United States.

The stories are basically the same. Usually, a perfectly healthy, happy baby is settled down for a little nap or bedtime without any hint of anything amiss. When the mother goes in to wake up infant, she finds her child dead, blue and very still. Resuscitation is attempted, the ambulance called, and the baby arrives in an Emergency Department, where doctors try to resurrect the infant. The tiny hope of life that was the baby has been extinguished, and no one knows why.

Three quarters of the deaths occur in infants between the ages of two and four months, and it is rare after ten months of age. SIDS is commoner in male than in female babies, in smaller babies and premature ones, in sibling of previous victims of SIDS, in infants born to mothers who smoked during their pregnancy, in families where cigarette smoke is found regularly in the home, in the offspring of mothers who are very young, and in Native Americans. The deaths most often occur during the cold season in temperature climates. One half of the infants have some sort of mild upper respiratory infection prior to death.

Significantly, SIDS occurs more frequently when infants are allowed to sleep in a prone or face down position and when infants are more heavily wrapped. The combination of viral illness, heavy wrapping, and the prone position increases the risk for SIDS tremendously. In New Zealand, where SIDS rates are inexplicably high, a campaign to educate mothers has resulted in a dramatic decrease in incidence almost 50 percent over two years.

SIDS may be sleep disorder, though the evidence is not conclusive. Most SIDS deaths occur either during the night or during nap time, suggesting a relationship with sleep. Parents who happened to be in the same room with their child at the time of death most often report that no crying was heard, raising the suspicion that the death may have occurred during sleep. We know that the ability to react to low oxygen levels in the blood is reduced during REM sleep, and the percentage of REM sleep is much higher in young infants that it is in older children and adults. We also know that sleep disturbances, including apnea, are commoner in premature infants who again have a greater amount of REM sleep. All these observations suggest that SIDS may be related to sleep.

When SIDS infants are examined carefully at autopsy, the only consistent finding is that of small groupings of fresh bruises on microscopic areas of blessing on the lungs and the lining of the heart. Exactly the same pattern is seen n infants who die in choking spells or from obstruction of their upper airway, suggesting that the final mechanism for SIDS may be the same.

However, conclusive evidence linking SIDS to a sleep disorder is lacking. Much of the clinically observed information doesn't fit this hypothesis, and the suspicious is that the phenomenon is much more complicated that a simple sleep disorder, though it may occurs during sleep.

How To Treat Colic The Natural Way

There are no drugs that can cure the child of colic, so parents will have to deal with it as effectively as they can, using natural remedies which can help soothe the infant.

Music is a wonderful way of soothing the child. If you don't have a tuneful voice, perhaps you can play music which can be kept near the crib so that the baby can fall asleep.

Something else that needs to be looked into is the food consumed by the mother - there are foods that contain gas and this can be passed on to the baby through the mother's milk. A dietician should be consulted so as to advise the mother on the foods that would be agreeable to the baby.

If the baby is not breast fed, then soy milk could be tried instead of the usual baby milk, and this could help with colic.

In addition to breast milk, babies need water - you will have to be careful and check the ingredients written on the package to make sure that your baby is not allergic to any of them.

The usual practice is to carry a baby when it screams, but when this becomes tiring, it would be a good idea to take the baby out of the house.

The baby can be taken in a stroller or firmly strapped in the car so that he can have a restful time with his mother in a park or just go for a ride in the car.

Just as adults enjoy a warm bath after work, babies could do with a bath that is warm, not hot, or aroma therapy will soothe the child by placing a warm bag on the infant's stomach.

After the baby has been in the mother's womb for 9 months, it is baffling for the infant to face the world with its sounds. Keeping a baby close to your breast or wrapping him warmly will help the baby adjust.

These natural methods will help but not always, so there are always ways of trying different things to comfort your child.

There are many medications available but you will need to use them only in consultation with your doctor.

If your child is diagnosed as colic, there is no cause for alarm as it is a normal process and not a disorder. Parents should be prepared to give up their sleep in order to comfort their child and make him feel secure.

CHAPTER 6- FOODS AND NATURAL HERBS TO HELP BABIES SLEEP

To help your child get a better night's sleep it's essential to have a relaxing evening and bedtime routine. Watching television or using computers or tablets before bed can make it much harder to fall asleep easily. This is because the blue light that is emitted by electronics causes the body to delay release of melatonin, the hormone responsible for making us sleepy at night. Instead of spending time on electronics, taking a bath and reading bedtime stories can help your child to relax and get ready for sleep.

Eating or drinking things with sugar and caffeine in the evening can also make it difficult for your child to sleep soundly. Sugar and caffeine have a stimulating effect on the body and can lead to hyperactivity in kids. If your child needs an evening snack, try something that includes complex carbohydrates, protein, and healthy fats. Some examples you might try are carrots and hummus, whole-wheat toast or crackers with peanut butter, or apple slices with almond butter. Combining nutrients in this way helps to prevent the highs and lows in energy and mood that can come from sugary and processed foods.

Here are five of my favorite natural treatments that may help:

Chamomile

Chamomile (Matricaria chamomilla, Matricaria recutita) is my favorite all around herb for kids. Historically, it has been used to treat everything from colds, teething pain, colic, indigestion, restlessness, anxiety, and irritability. It is the perfect herb for cranky infants and children who can't settle down enough to fall sleep. Chamomile tea is readily available from many grocery and natural health stores. A small amount of honey can be added for children over 12 months old to make the tea even tastier. Chamomile is generally considered very safe, but because it is in the Asteraceae (i.e. daisy) family it should not be given to anyone with an allergy to other plants in this family.

Magnesium

Magnesium is a naturally occurring mineral and an essential nutrient. Magnesium has a calming effect on the nervous system and may help to promote restful sleep. A good dosage for most children ages 2 to 8 year old is 100 mg of magnesium at bedtime. The recommended upper daily limit for older children and adults is 350 mg. More is not always better and if you ingest too much magnesium it can cause abdominal pain, cramping, diarrhea, and low blood pressure.

The type of magnesium in your supplements can also make a big difference! Magnesium supplements are often prepared by combining magnesium with organic and amino acids in order to make them more chemically stable and to improve absorption. The type of organic acid that the magnesium is mixed with can alter of the effects of the supplement. For example, magnesium citrate and magnesium oxide tend to have laxative effects, which your child may or may not need. Magnesium glycinate has the least laxative effect and it may be a good choice for people with sensitive digestive systems. Other common forms of magnesium include magnesium malate, magnesium aspartate, and magnesium threonate.

California Poppy

California Poppy (Eschscholzia californica) is a very gentle herb to calm the nervous system. It is useful for restlessness, pain, and sleeplessness. Although related to other types of poppies, California Poppy does NOT contain opium or opiates and it is very safe for kids over the age of 2 years. California Poppy is included in a lot of calming herbal formulas, including one of my favorites: Wise Woman Herbals Kalmerite Glycerite.

Lavender

Just the smell of lavender (Lavandula angustifolia) is relaxing to most people and it's widely used in aromatherapy to calm the nervous system and promote restful sleep. Lavender bath products can be before bed or you can spritz a few drops of organic lavender essential oil on your child's pillowcase. You can also involve your child in a fun craft project to make lavender dream pillows.

When using essential oils don't apply them directly to the skin because they can be irritating or even cause chemical burns. Use extra caution when using essential oils around infants and children who have asthma.

Regular Physical Activity

Okay, so it's not really a "treatment," but if your child spends a lot of time sitting still during the day they may not be sleeping as well at night. Our bodies needs regular physical movement and exercise to burn off energy so that we are tired enough to sleep well at night. A good goal is to make sure your child is getting at least 30 minutes of unstructured outdoor time every day to run around. Getting them involved in sports, gymnastics, martial arts, or other group exercise programs can also be helpful.

Although sleep issues are very common and often relatively harmless, if your child experiences chronic insomnia it may be related to a more serious medical condition and you should consult your family doctor. Sleep disorders in children and adolescents can be a sign of anxiety, depression, ADHD, thyroid disease, sleep apnea, and even asthma.

Do Solid Foods Help the Baby Sleep Longer?

It was once thought that solid foods should be offered to infants within the first month or two of life. Although such young infants are unable to swallow much of the food offered (most of it ends up on their faces and bibs), or to digest completely what they do swallow, solid foods were thought to fill the baby up and help him or her sleep through the night. Giving solid foods before the age of four months does not accomplish that. Infants who are fed solids early are no more likely to sleep through the night than are those who start to eat solid foods between four and six months of age. The age at which an infant begins to sleep for six or more hours during the night depends on other factors, including the infant's developmental level and how much she or he has slept during the day. Neither the infant nor the parents are likely to get a good night's sleep for at least four months.

Feeding Infants in the Second Six Months of Life

Strained meats (chicken, turkey, beef, and pork) and legumes (cooked dried beans and peas) are good foods to introduce between six and seven months. By the time an infant is seven months old, he or she is ready to chew or to gum and swallow foods with a bit of texture. Offering textured foods at this time helps the baby learn to chew and swallow and appears to foster the development of speaking skills. Foods offered should be the consistency of thick soup and contain lumpy pieces of soft food. Although you can purchase baby foods of the right consistency, you can also make them at home using a food mill or food processor.

Finger foods should also be introduced when the baby is seven months old. Foods offered should be easy to pick up, not re□uire much chewing, and be in small enough pieces so that they can be easily swallowed.

By nine months of age, infants are ready for mashed and finely cut-up foods. Infants graduate to adult-type foods toward the end of the first year of life. Although most foods still need to be mashed or cut up into small pieces, one-year-olds are able to eat the same types of foods as the rest of the family. They can drink from a cup and nearly feed themselves with a spoon. Infants have come a long way in twelve months!

Do Infants Need Vitamin or Mineral Supplements?

Two situations call for the use of supplements during infancy. Breastfed infants and infants receiving formula from a concentrate not diluted with fluoridated water need fluoride supplements after six months of age. Since breast milk contains a low amount of vitamin D, breast-fed infants not exposed regularly to sunshine should receive 5 µg (200 IU) vitamin D as a daily supplement. Babies who are exposed to sunshine thirty minutes per week while in diapers only, or two hours per week if only the head is exposed, make enough vitamin D in their skin. Care should be taken to ensure the baby isn't overexposed to sunshine.

Sunbathing infants in the indirect rays of the sun in the morning and late afternoon is best in the summer months. Periods of direct exposure to sunshine without sunscreen should be brief, ten minutes or less at a time.

There is nothing like the feel and smell of your baby. It is what bonds Mother and child. The most common way to calm a fussy child is to pick them up and cuddle. It is a psychological and physiological need in every human. It is important to have that human contact, the feel of skin to skin. It is a part of the development and socialization of a baby.

Massaging your baby can be relaxing and stimulating at the same time. How can that be, you ask. Even babies have certain levels of stress even though they don't really do anything and can't watch the news to obtain outside stresses. One of the most stressful things for a baby is to be separated from its mother or care giver. When mother and child are reunited after a work day often the first thing the mother will do is to hug the baby. This reassures the baby and calms the mother too.

The initial contact with mother will calm and relax the child but how is it stimulating? Babies' muscles are not developed and can only become useful through use and control. When massaging a baby, you are making that baby aware of their different body parts. They might not realize what is down there or what they can do with it. Massage and exercise of the baby's legs will strengthen them for the time when the baby will crawl or walk. Even a very young baby can try to extend their legs and stand or bounce when held. They same is true for the babies arms. It can also develop better hand to eye coordination. Even though most babies are good at getting things into their mouths, there are different tasks they may enjoy when they can control their limbs.

A mother should develop a routine for massage. A good time is in the evening after a bath. For some babies, bath time can be very stressful even if they do it every day. Afterward the mother can lay the baby down and massage baby oil or lotion into its skin. This is soothing and calming for the baby and good for the baby's skin too. There are also scented baby oils that can be used to calm. In recent years the use of lavender scented products has become a popular way to provide aromatherapy for infants.

After the baby has been massaged and dressed it is time for the final feeding. After the feeding it is best to hold the baby close and rock them, rubbing and patting their back can eliminate any gassy build up that can prevent the baby from sleeping well. When done properly the baby should feel very relaxed and assured from the parent and sleep well.

Benefits of massaging your baby

Massaging your Baby brings enormous benefits to both the Baby and to the person giving the massage. Touch is the most important of all our senses. It is critical to our well-being, and is so important that our growth and development relies on it.

Massage is a rather broad term and can include many types of touch such as stroking and holding. It does not designate a particular set of movements. There are as many forms of Baby Massage as there are Babies.

What are the benefits of Massaging your Baby?

(For the purpose of this book, I have been using mother, but it of course can be father, grandpa or any other person who massages the Baby)

1. Relaxation

Both Mother and Baby receive this bonus. Endorphins (the 'happy hormones') are released, and these stop us from feeling anxious and give us feelings of pleasure and well-being.

2. Helps the bonding process

Nurturing touch grows confidence and trust in the Baby. Eye contact during the massage encourages the formation of a good relationship between the baby and the massage giver.

3. Connection

The gentle touch, eye contact, talk and smell of the massage person, all help form a two-way connection which gives the Baby a secure base.

4. Comfort

Constipation may be relieved by gentle tummy massage -Crying is often reduced by massage. -Grizzly and Fussy babies often calm with regular massage -The discomfort of teething may be helped by the general relaxation -This means less pain for the Baby and less Anxiety for the Mother.

5. Sleep

Babies sleep longer and deeper when they have massage regularly.

6. Enhanced Development

The Baby grows stronger, both emotionally and physically - Massage encourages movement and coordination. -Massage helps babies to stretch and move, and to discover their abilities and bodies. -Mental and motor skills are improved. -Circulation and digestive systems are boosted. -Massage helps strengthen joints and muscles.

7. Stimulation of Immune system

Production of Cortisol and other Stress hormones is reduced, so Stress is relieved. Massage can encourage the removal of waste and toxins from the body.

8. Less Post-Natal Depression

The relaxation of the Mother and the Baby makes for less mental load for the Mother to deal with. Baby massage can be a very enjoyable experience for both the baby and parents.

It should be a truly enjoyable experience for both, and if it is not, then the massage should not continue.

The likelihood is that the whole experience of having a Baby to care for will be much smoother and more delightful.

Less anxiety in Mother and Baby is going to make it much comfortable for everyone.

Massaging Your Baby - Techni☐ues for Mother and Baby
When to Massage

Massaging can be done as often as you like, as long as it is enjoyable for both baby and you! In the beginning, your newborn may only like a massage to last for a few minutes, but with time, the baby will enjoy longer sessions. Choose times when your baby is relaxed. When your baby is laying ☐uietly, and prior to your baby's usual crying time or prior to bedtime. Just after a bath can be very relaxing for baby, and if you use Chamomile and Lavender in your massage oil, it will help promote a restful sleep. Even when feeding, you can take the opportunity to massage baby's little hands and feet, or gently stroke the face and head.

When Not to Massage:

If baby is unwell or has a high temperature

After immunisation - do not massage for at least 48 hours

Baby has any cuts or wounds

If baby has had a medical procedure

What to Use

Always be mindful of the ingredients that you are applying to your baby's sensitive skin. The newborn's skin is more absorbent because the outer layers are not yet fully developed, so any product that you apply, will have an effect on their health. Read your product labels carefully and become familiar with those ingredients that may be harmful, such as:

paraben

sodium laureth sulphate

sodium lauryl sulphate

PEG's

petro chemicals

mineral oils

grape seed extract

Choose a pure natural carrier oil, that is nourishing for the skin, such as Sweet Almond Oil, Sunflower Oil or Apricot Kernel Oil. With the addition of Essential Oils, you can add to the benefits your baby will receive from each massage. You only need to add 5 drops of Essential Oil to 100 ml of carrier oil, and always perform a skin test on your baby first to ensure no adverse reactions occur. Apply a small amount of oil to a very small area of skin. Wait for 30 minutes, and if there is no irritations or reaction, then you are ready to go!

Here are some perfect Essential Oils to add to your carrier oil:

Chamomile - soothing, calming and restful, and calming for over tired children

Lavender - relaxing, calming, healing

Mandarin - cheery, soothing, antiseptic, refreshing

Rose - sedative, soothing, anti-inflammatory, soothing for the skin

How to Massage

Being attentive to your baby's likes and dislikes will make the way you approach your massage routine more enjoyable and effective for you both. Massage is most beneficial when your baby is naked, but some babies do not like this, so they may prefer to be clothed or with just a singlet. Ensure that the room is warm, and is free from any distraction, such as phones, television or other noise. Take a moment to relax, and to calm yourself. Also have your hands nice and warm before you commence, as you do not want to startle baby with a cold touch.

Newborn Babies

An excellent position for starting your massage routine for a newborn, is to lie on your side facing baby. Then with a warm, well oiled hand, start with the upper back, in a clockwise, circular motion. Stay here for about a minute, and remember to use slow strokes, keeping continuous contact with the skin. Then gradually move down to massage baby's hips, and base of the spine for another minute. To complete this incredible experience, lie on your back, and gently lift baby onto your tummy. Skin on skin would, at this stage, provide the most effective bonding experience. Now, continue the massage, hand over hand, down baby's back, on both sides of the spine, again for approximately one minute.

Baby's from 6 weeks

From around six weeks of age, when baby is happy to lay on their back, you can introduce an all over body routine. Using the same soft circular strokes, start with the soles of the feet, from heels towards toes. Use long smooth strokes for the whole leg, from the ankle to the thigh area. From here move to the shoulders, using both hands move with circular strokes toward the chest. Massage the arms also using long strokes from the shoulders to the wrists. At this stage do not add oil to baby's hands or fingers, as they may put this into their mouth. If baby's tummy is not hard or full, then massage using your circular motions. Tummy's can be sensitive, so if your baby seems to become unsettled when you are massaging this area, then stop and move onto the next area. If you feel confident, then commence massaging the face by starting will little circles from the middle of the forehead, down the cheeks. With your fingertips, lightly massage baby's head, as if to be shampooing hair. If your baby is still happy, then turn them over and finish the session with long smooth strokes from head to toe.

Your massage sessions should not be rushed, and should always be an enjoyable experience for you both. Points to remember are:

Warm hands, that are well lubricated

Have a warm room and ensure baby is warm

Don't wake your baby for a massage

Be aware, if baby cries, stop, as the baby may have other needs that need to be attended to first

Keep your strokes smooth and continuous, and repeat each stroke several times

Do not force baby's limbs into position

And enjoy the time with your very special little person.

CHAPTER 8- COMMON SENSE BEDDING ADVICE FOR NEW MOTHERS

When it comes to baby bedding, it would be best to put beauty aside for shopping and careful research for now, no matter how tempting it may be. You're probably wondering why the utmost care is needed when shopping for baby nursery crib bedding. Since your baby is going to spend a lot of his time surrounded in bedding, you need to make sure that every blanket and sheet is made of top quality material, which is both safe and gentle enough for your baby to sleep and play in. Plus, choosing baby bedding that will not irritate the sensitive skin of your baby or give him allergies would be extremely essential to encourage him to fall asleep soundly.

Here are some tips to consider when choosing baby bedding for your newborn angel:

Quality Is More Important Than Price. In a lot of cases in baby articles shopping, parents opt for items that are cheaper to save themselves some money; however, with baby nursery crib bedding, quality should definitely be more important than price. The skin of your baby will always be in contact with crib bedding, so you should opt for bedding material that is both warm and soft, as well as made out of top quality material, which will not irritate your baby's sensitive skin. Budget sets of baby nursery bedding are usually made out of cheap synthetic material of low quality that could make your baby fuss out of irritation to his sensitive skin. Be wary of such types of bedding sets. Although they are cheap, they won't save you a lot of money in the long run.

Look for Proper Material. While looking for top quality set of bedding, it would be important to opt for baby bedding made out of lighter material, so your baby won't overheat during the summer. Cotton would be the ideal choice in bedding material since it will let your baby breathe easier, as well as sleep more soundly without interrupting his sleep cycle due to too much warmth.

Match Your Theme. After covering your bedding budget and getting rid of possible safety hazards, it would be high time to concentrate on having fun while shopping: choosing patterns or colors that will fit your nursery's theme for girl crib bedding or boy crib bedding. If you don't have a nursery theme yet since you don't know your baby's gender, opt for neutral colors like yellow or green when it comes to your set of baby nursery bedding. A lot of different patterns could inspire your theme, as well. So, if you see a pattern that you are interested in, plan your nursery around that pattern.

Go Green. Although a lot of parents opt for more organic materials in life, there are still tons of people out there that aren't interested in organic baby bedding. It would be important to keep in mind that organic bedding is usually purchased since it is made without irritants or chemicals that might afflict the baby's health. Organic material is completely allergen-free and a lot of parents are more comfortable knowing that their baby is surrounded by soft materials from Mother Nature.

Choosing the ideal set of baby bedding should revolve solely around your baby's ultimate comfort and safety. This way, you will both sleep better as your baby rests in ultra-soft top □uality bedding of your choice.

Tips For Selecting The Best Baby Sleep Wear

There's just something so indescribable about the look on a new baby's face, the touch of their tiny hands and the warm, cuddling embrace. Before we even have a chance to take a deep breath, they own us entirely, forever and always.

Then, of course, panic sets in!

We moms worry about everything! From selecting correct toys to trying to decide if their rooms are decorated just right. If it has to do with our new bundles of joy, it's an issue that's worth fretting over.

There are just too many things to think of.

When it comes to baby sleep wear, there are some excellent suggestions to help make sure you get it right.

Selecting the best sleepwear is not rocket science. But it is serious business which can cost you a lot of money and valuable sleep if you get it wrong.

Great big blankets, hot, fuzzy sleepers and other overpowering sleep wear generally is not the way to go.

In fact, the American SIDs Institute offers some very simple advice. That organization says basic, comfortable baby sleep wear that doesn't overheat is generally the best route to take.

When coupled with a room that is kept at a comfortable temperature your little bundle of joy should sleep like a lamb.

So, what exactly does this mean?

It means applying a little old fashion commonsense to the selection of sleep wear. Some basic ideas to consider include:

* Swaddle blankets. There are some fantastic wearable sleep blankets that are ideal for newborns that like a snug feel. They are especially great in cooler climates or when indoor temperatures are kept a little low for adults' comfort.

The Halo Sleep Sack is an example of these. The beauty of this particular option is that it replaces the need for often dangerous loose-fitting blankets. When coupled with a one-piece sleeper, these safer blankets are often ideal.

* Basic sleepers. Footed sleepers and even Onesie-type body suits are quite often ideal for cooler and warmer temperatures, respectively. Just make sure the materials selected breathe and are not too snug or too loose fitting.

* Nightgowns. While these are always popular, nightgowns can be a pain in the neck for wiggly newborns and older infants. If she likes to scoot around, they can bunch up and cause some problems. Use your best judgment here.

* Thickness, buttons and other concerns. Make sure baby sleep wear is not too thick and hot. Also, check for any pieces that might come off and cause choking hazards. Buttons are cute, but unless they are very, very big, they probably do not belong on your sleep wear.

* Materials. The fabrics involved in creating baby sleep wear are worth worrying about. Make sure they are non-flammable or at least flame

retardant. Even the best-selected wardrobe of baby clothes can turn out a mistake if the wrong materials go into their creation.

Moms are worriers and rightfully so. When it comes to selecting the right clothes, fortunately there are ways to put some of the concerns to rest.

Apply a little common sense, read the labels and try to relax. This is one area where getting it right isn't that difficult.

CONCLUSION

For many parents of newborns, putting them to sleep can seem like a colossal task that affects the entire household. You start thinking about how one little person can affect everybody else's sleeping patterns by not having sleeping patterns of his own! Well, you simply must exercise more patience when putting your baby to sleep as well as practice ingenious ways to do so.

Make Sleepy Time Restful

Babies can be made to follow routines by providing them with strong associations. Thus, if you want to make your baby sleep at a certain time, you must provide the motivation for him to relax and then sleep. You must set relaxing activities before putting him to sleep. Play soothing lullabies for him, give him a gentle massage and coo to him softly, all of which will provide the right atmosphere of relaxation.

In essence, you are providing him with the opportunity to wind down. As such, it is advisable to make his room dim so that he may not be stimulated by the colorful patterns on the walls or the play of light on the ceiling. You may also provide warm baths for him except during nap times. Just make sure that it relaxes him because some babies do become more active when baths are provided for them just before sleepy time!

Remove Distractions

While it may not be possible or advisable to remove all distractions from the room, it is an excellent idea to make sure that your baby finds no reason to stay awake. Your other children must be well out of the nursery, sources of loud noises like the radio and the television must not be heard from the room and the lights are turned down low. This way, you and your baby can focus on letting him fall asleep. If you are breastfeeding him before putting him down to sleep, you must nurse in a ☐uiet part of the room. However, it is a good idea to provide soft, soothing music so that any inadvertent loud noises will not startle him so easily and on he goes to dreamland.

Keep It Regular

Although your baby may not seem to have regular sleeping patterns now - it changes as he grows in terms of the number of hours slept and the day of time favored for sleeping - you can make his sleepy time as regular as possible. Again, this is possible if you can adopt regular and relaxing bedtime routines.

Probably one of the most relaxing bedtime routines is rocking your baby to sleep. It mimics the atmosphere in your womb, which speeds up his relaxation. Don't be afraid to do this despite the fear of others that your baby will not fall asleep without you rocking him to sleep during his older years. Keep in mind that he is still a baby and deserves all the soothing a mother and father can give him. After all, he is braving a new world and it is the parents' job to soothe his fears.

Many mothers have the maternal instinct to have their baby sleep with them in their own bed. This is natural instinct, originating from times when babies were fair game for nocturnal predators, but these are uncommon in normal urban environments. In some areas of the world, it is still valid, but modern mothers should restrict this to having the child sleep in the same room at first.

This is fine: it allows you to tend to your baby during the night without too much disruption and your baby will find a sleep pattern much quicker knowing his mother is close by.

I do not recommend parents sleeping with their babies. It may work for some, but there have been tragic cases. Young babies are too weak to struggle if a parent rolls over onto them, and there have been cases of suffocation occurring in this way.

There is also the question of whether a baby should sleep on his stomach or his back. The normal advice given is that Sudden Infant Death Syndrome (SIDS) is more prevalent with children put to bed on their stomach than on their back. I am making no inference here, but these are the facts. I personally would choose to place my child on his back at bedtime. After a few months he will be strong enough to roll about and choose his own most comfortable sleeping position.

A bassinet, pram or Moses basket by your bed is a suitable bed for your baby in the early days. You will be less disturbed while feeding, and your child will feel more secure. Children know when their mothers are close by. They can sense you and smell you. If you are breast feeding you will be able to feed your child without leaving your bed: this will help to prevent you from being grumpy during the day. Good for your baby and good for your partner!

Once your baby is around three months old she can be put in a crib to sleep in her own room. It should be achieved gradually, with the light on and with a feed and a cuddle first and you will have to return to the room several times a night for the first few weeks. Some children manage this younger and some take a bit longer, but it will be achieved ⊔uicker if you take the above advice. There is no real 'right way' of getting your baby to sleep, but this advice is based on what is known to succeed.

Eventually, your child will get used to it and will settle down, and though a night light normally keeps them more at ease, you have achieved your objective of getting baby to sleep through the night.

Putting your baby to sleep need not be a task for the Titans. You must take great joy in it for there will come a time when your child will not allow you to tuck him in and then you will miss the times when he was dependent on you for bedtime.

Printed in Great Britain
by Amazon

43258144R00040